Wuthering Heights

Journal Notebook

Lunar Glow Readers
PUBLISHING

Made in the USA
Middletown, DE
13 March 2022

62597882R00057